Read for a
Better World™

HOCKEY
A First Look

KATIE PETERS

GRL Consultant, Diane Craig, Certified Literacy Specialist

Lerner Publications ◆ Minneapolis

Educator Toolbox

Reading books is a great way for kids to express what they're interested in. Before reading this title, ask the reader these questions:

> What do you think this book is about? Look at the cover for clues.
>
> What do you already know about hockey?
>
> What do you want to learn about hockey?

Let's Read Together

Encourage the reader to use the pictures to understand the text.

Point out when the reader successfully sounds out a word.

Praise the reader for recognizing sight words such as *in* and *at*.

TABLE OF CONTENTS

Hockey 4

Hockey

Many kids play hockey.
They play in fall
and winter.

ice skates

You need ice skates.

You need a helmet.

helmet

You need a hockey stick.
You need a puck.

hockey stick ←   → **puck**

Two teams play.
They play on the ice.
Each team has
a goal.

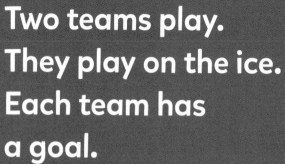

Have you ever gone ice skating?

Players hit the puck with their sticks.

**Why do players
need helmets?**

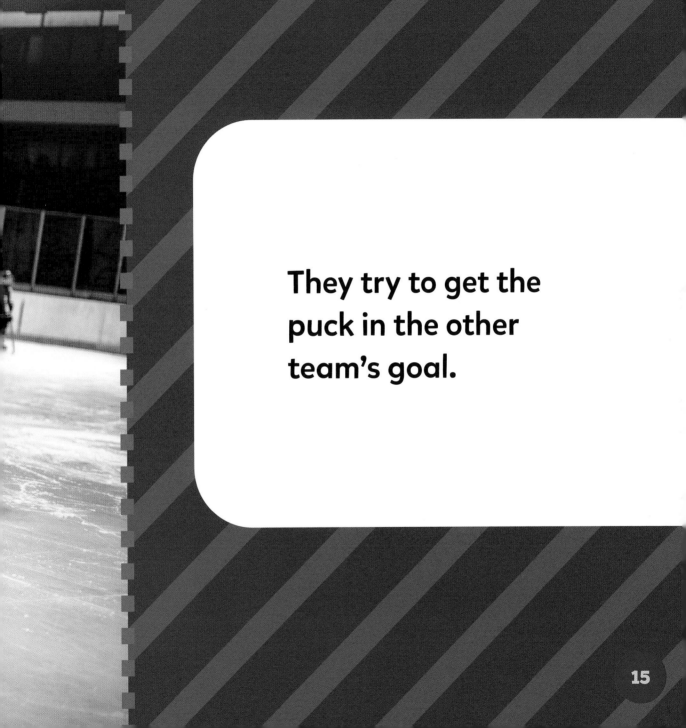

They try to get the
puck in the other
team's goal.

The puck slides
to the goal.
The goalie tries
to stop it.

What other sports have goals?

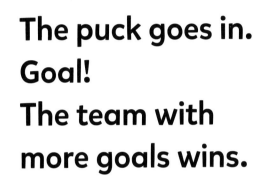

The puck goes in.
Goal!
The team with
more goals wins.

Players and fans have fun
at hockey games.

You Connect!

Have you ever played hockey before?

What part of a hockey game seems most fun to you?

How could you get better at playing hockey?

Social and Emotional Snapshot

Student voice is crucial to building reader confidence. Ask the reader:

What is your favorite part of this book?

What is something you learned from this book?

Did this book remind you of any sports you play?

Opportunities for social and emotional learning are everywhere. How can you connect the topic of this book to the SEL competencies below?

Responsible Decision-Making
Self-Awareness
Self-Management

Photo Glossary

goal

goalie

ice skates

puck

Learn More

Gigliotti, Jim. *Talkin' Hockey*. Mankato, MN: The Child's World, 2020.

Haley, Charly. *Hockey*. Minneapolis: Pop!, 2020.

Sabino, David. *Slap Shot*. New York: Simon & Schuster, 2019.

Index

Photo Acknowledgments

The images in this book are used with the permission of: © emholk/iStockphoto, pp. 4–5; © marieclaudelemay/iStockphoto, pp. 6, 23 (ice skates); © FatCamera/iStockphoto, p. 7; © Kat72/Shutterstock Images, pp. 8–9, 23 (puck); © DardaInna/Shutterstock Images, pp. 10–11, 23 (goal); © Ideas_Studio/iStockphoto, p. 10; © ImagineGolf/iStockphoto, pp. 12–13; © LuckyBusiness/iStockphoto, pp. 14–15; © bigjohn36/iStockphoto, pp. 16–17, 18–19, 23 (goalie); © Lucky Business/Shutterstock Images, p. 20.

Cover Photograph: © FamVeld/iStockphoto.

Design Elements: © Mighty Media, Inc.

Lerner Publications Company
An imprint of Lerner Publishing Group, Inc.
241 First Avenue North
Minneapolis, MN 55401 USA

For reading levels and more information, look up this title at www.lernerbooks.com.

Main body text set in Mikado a Medium.
Typeface provided by Hannes von Doehren.

Library of Congress Cataloging-in-Publication Data

Names: Peters, Katie, author.
Title: Hockey : a first look / Katie Peters.
Description: Minneapolis, MN : Lerner Publications, 2023. | Series: Read about sports. Read for a better world | Includes bibliographical references and index. | Audience: Ages 5–8 | Audience: Grades K–1 | Summary: "Hockey is a fun fall and winter sport. Learn about equipment, rules, and more in this thrilling introduction to the game"— Provided by publisher.
Identifiers: LCCN 2022011587 (print) | LCCN 2022011588 (ebook) | ISBN 9781728475721 (library binding) | ISBN 9781728479057 (paperback) | ISBN 9781728484549 (ebook)
Subjects: LCSH: Hockey—Juvenile literature.
Classification: LCC GV847.25 .P486 2023 (print) | LCC GV847.25 (ebook) | DDC 796.962092—dc23/eng/20220201

LC record available at https://lccn.loc.gov/2022011587
LC ebook record available at https://lccn.loc.gov/2022011588

Manufactured in the United States of America
1 – CG – 12/15/22